Leadership Made Easy

**Empowering Yourself And Your Team - Essential Guide
For Leadership**

By: William "Bill" Groves

9781635010015

I0500257

PUBLISHERS NOTES

Disclaimer – Speedy Publishing LLC

Speedy Publishing LLC

40 E Main Street, Newark, Delaware, 19711

Contact Us: 1-888-248-4521

Website: http://www.speedypublishing.co

REPRINTED Paperback Edition: ISBN: 9781635010015

Manufactured in the United States of America

DEDICATION

I dedicate this book to my only son, Josh. You bring the best in me and inspired me to do more.

TABLE OF CONTENTS

Chapter 1 - Leadership Management Starts In You

Napoleon once said: "One bad general does better than two good ones." It takes a moment for the sense of this to register, but it is the same as our modern saying that "too many cooks spoil the broth". Having one set of instructions, even if they are flawed, is preferable to having two sets of perfect directions that, when enacted together without reference to each other, cause havoc.

This is the principle of leadership in a nutshell. It is all about maintaining focus and creating positive outcomes.

The same can be applied to individuals who strive to become leaders. There needs to be focus and determination. Advice can be given, but does not have to be heeded. History is full of leaders whose beginnings were disastrous, and had they listened to the naysayers of this world, the world would be a poorer place today.

Leadership can be learned. Some people are certainly born with leadership skills, but this is not a prerequisite for becoming a leader. More important is dedication to the art of leadership. Leadership involves understanding how to inspire, influence and control how people behave. It is not a simple matter of shouting, or having a deep and booming voice; or being great in physical stature; Gandhi possessed none of these attributes, but managed to lead a nation and inspire millions around the world.

Sometimes, leadership may be no more than having a poignant message for a receptive audience at an opportune moment. Of itself, leadership is neither good nor bad; the world has known more than its fair share of evil and charismatic dictators.

In the world of business, the perception of leadership has changed from its early days when it largely mirrored the military model of leadership from the top down, with powerful individuals dominating large groups of less powerful people.

Nowadays, leadership in business is far more knowledge-driven. The lowliest employee may end up effectively leading the direction of a vast corporation through his or her innovative ideas. Anyone with critical knowledge can show leadership. This is known as thought-leadership. In other situations, leadership can be about taking a stand for what you believe in, and trying to convince people to think and act differently.

Leadership has been variously described as the "process of social influence in which one person can enlist the aid and support of others in the accomplishment of a common task"; "creating a way for people to contribute to making something extraordinary happen"; "the ability to successfully integrate and maximize available resources within the internal and external environment for the attainment of organizational or societal goals"; and "the capacity of leaders to listen and observe, to use their expertise as a starting point to encourage dialogue between all levels of decision-making, to establish processes and transparency in decision-making, to articulate their own values and visions clearly but not impose them. Leadership is about setting and not just reacting to agendas, identifying problems, and initiating change that makes for substantive improvement rather than managing change".

There is truth to all of the above definitions, but they all apply to the ideals of leadership.

So what of leadership gone awry?

Chapter 2- How to be a Good Follower and a Good Leader?

Leading people has nothing to do with managing them. Too many managers are trying to micro-manage their staff, all the while forgetting to lead them effectively.

If you want to become a strong leader you need to lead by example. This means you have to show your team that you are perfectly capable to set examples. By doing so, you will earn their respect and create lifelong devotees who would move mountains to please you.

A manager who hides behind his office door while commanding staff, isn't going to gain much respect in the work place.

Ultimately the success of any business venture lies in the hands of its employees and NOT the managers. A manager's responsibility is to organize and manage business systems, systems that will see to the successful finalization of projects.

If your staff is unhappy it will soon show in their lack of productivity. This will influence your bottom line. Chances are customer complaints will start to amass and office gossip will run hot. This is counterproductive to running a well oiled machine – your business.

No organization can function for very long without the co-operation of its employees. Unfortunately, the necessity in any organization is that there are various levels of status within the team, and this can lead to conflicts if not managed properly.

The effective leader has to realize that the team under them is there because they have to be. Most employees work to earn money, not because they enjoy the daily grind of a nine-to-five.

For this reason, there must be an effort to build healthy relationships, or life in the workplace can become untenable for everyone, and productivity will decline.

Leaders need to make their workplace society function positively, with co- operation and respect. In this way everyone is working for the common good and towards a common purpose. This demands that effective relationships are built upon an understanding of each other's needs. It is no different to how things should be in the home; no personal relationship will last very long if there is a sense that one or both parties are being selfish.

The most effective way to understand how other people are feeling is to listen to what they have to say. This must be done without judging, and not as though you are being forced to do so by some higher authority. Very often, teams will have the same goals as their leaders, but may just want to know that they are not seen as automatons that have no creative input.

Quality workplace relationships make people feel happy. One of the major reasons why employees move on from a company is because of relationship clashes with leaders or other colleagues.

Leaders should also make sure that they create the circumstances for understanding within their team, and this means asking questions. Assuming that your team will simply pipe up and express their feelings is not enough; many people will not feel it is their place to speak up unless they are specifically asked to do so.

Listening should be done attentively, not glancing at your watch every couple of minutes or trying not to look bored. This means you listen without interrupting or fidgeting, and with the correct expression. Your expression, by the way, should be genuine or you will be found out very quickly and the situation will become worse than had you not asked in the first place.

A great way to foster healthy relationships with your team is by meeting them in a more social environment on regular occasions. Some companies choose to send their staff to regular golfing outings while others prefer to host a monthly BBQ or weekend trips.

Regardless what you end up choosing, the key lies in giving your team a chance to connect away from the daily grind.

Building effective relationships means that neither party must make any assumptions. As a leader, you cannot expect people to understand exactly what we want and why you want it. Sometimes it is this lack of comprehension that causes problems. As much as you must trust your team members to have intelligence, if they are not party to the goals you are working towards they can become resistant. As far as possible, your team should be conversant with your goals and how their actions are contributing to their successful outcome. Humans are inquisitive and function better when not kept in the dark.

Respect is the key ingredient of any good relationship, and this means respect for yourself as well as others. Genuinely listening and understanding are the ways in which you show that you respect the person you are talking to.

Quickly judging based on preconceived ideas or prejudice is the opposite of having respect. Bear in mind that not everyone will respond in 100% perfect fashion to all that occurs in the workplace. Although it is not the leader's job to be a permanent shoulder to cry on, it is important to accept that your team is made up of individuals whose lives may not be as perfect as their coffee- break banter might lead you to believe.

Whilst creating a healthy working relationship is a crucial goal, the smart leader will always bear in mind that conflict is inevitable and must be managed, rather than ignored for the sake of apparent peace.

Chapter 3- Develop Your Leadership Skills and Empower Others

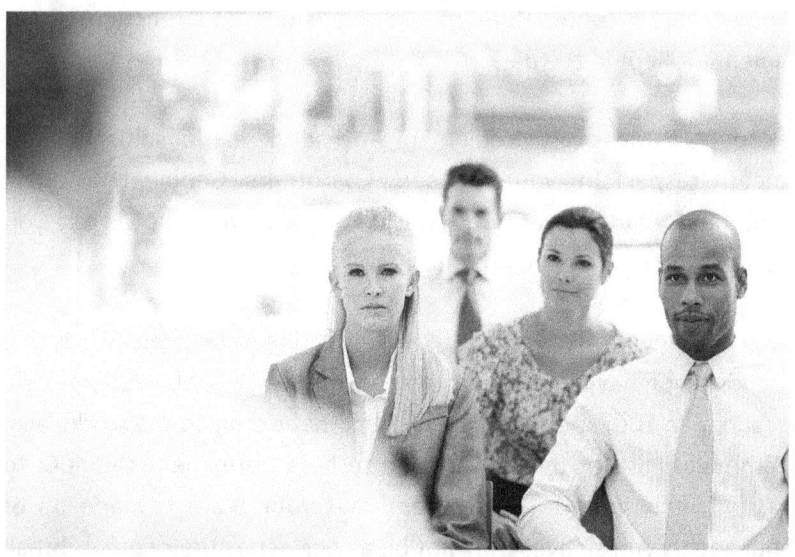

Leaders must take responsibility for their team's performance, which means leaders must be happy that the direction of their team is one which the leader thinks is best. Although it is useful to have creative sessions with team members to bat around a few ideas, the overarching goals that the team must fulfill are most often set by the leader, or some authority above the leader.

The challenge is therefore to get the team "onside" with the given aims, even when some team members may wholeheartedly disagree with them, or baulk at the idea that these have been imposed on them from above.

Despite the accepted hierarchy of any workplace, for a team to work most efficiently, its members – especially higher level ones – may want to feel they are contributing more than the spade work;

they may like to feel that they have chosen where some of the plots should be dug.

This presents a challenge for the leader who cannot just let his or her subordinates have free play. The team must be made to feel involved and motivated. Or perhaps the situation is worse, and your team is beginning to show a little disobedience. How then to provoke a positive response in them?

The answer is by empowering your team, as far as possible. Short of handing over the reins and heading off home, the motivational leader must be able to create a sense that their team is actively involved in the process and contributing in a real sense to the overall outcome of the project.

This can involve learning how to make your suggestions appeal to them. This may mean you solicit their opinions and take the best ideas on board. Or you may have to convince them that your goals are shared and that their futures are tied to your overall success. It may be a simple matter of making an employee understand that their job will be safer if they perform well; reminding them that they are working for themselves and their family, and not just for a company.

However, empowering others does not just mean employing tactics that persuade other people to your own opinion or goals. It can also mean demonstrating leadership qualities that inspire others to act at their very best, no matter what is asked of them. Such leadership qualities would be most in evidence in the armed services, where the end result of potentially being killed is rarely going to elicit a whoop and a cheer. Soldiers are empowered to greatness by the examples set by their commanding officers.

Sometimes, it is just a matter of being an admirable and inspirational human being. Of course, some are born with more of these qualities than others, but we can all strive to lead by example, so that others will feel empowered to make great things happen.

Getting the Most from Your Team Start right

When a staff member joins your team, give them time to become fully acclimatized to your company. The sooner they settle, the sooner you can start to reap rewards. It will help if you complete an induction and a detailed contract of employment, which outlines what you expect from them.

Create expectations

Strange as it may sound, some employees do not have a clear sense of their role. Such confusion can cause arguments, or even duplication or omission of tasks. This is clearly bad for productivity. Your team needs to know their job and responsibilities; a job description will help.

Stand back

Part of empowering your team is trusting that they can get on with the job without you peering over their shoulder every fifteen minutes. If you want staff members to flourish, they should be allowed to get on with their job.

Of course you need to keep a watchful eye, but there is a happy medium where they know you trust them. Your team is more likely to over-perform if they feel good about what they are doing. Motivated staff works harder. Money is often not the prime motivator. They want to know what is expected of them, and then they want to be allowed to get on with it. This is far easier if the right people are employed in the first place.

Communication

Effective communication is the lifeblood of any organization, regardless of its size. That may mean face-to-face talks or pinning notes on a board.

Provided your team knows what's going on, you are being an effective leader. Try asking your team how they prefer communication to happen. This helps to empower them.

Keep communicating

It can happen that there is a sincere intention to improve communication, and it all starts off positively: team briefs, newsletters; intranets, etc. Then things start to slow down. As a leader you should not let this happen. It may mean important information is not imparted, or you are viewed as not bothered how the team is getting on.

Be honest

Communication is not much use if your team believes it is not getting the whole picture. Bad news is still news, and you must trust that your people are mature enough to handle it, or you may find they are insulted and no longer believe what you tell them. This does not mean shouting every piece of office gossip from the rooftop, but it does mean keeping your team abreast of all that is pertinent to them.

Consultation

Effective consultation is a vital tool to improving performance. Your team members have specific roles. Your collective overview may be more knowledgeable, but there may be team members whose specific knowledge is greater than yours.

Asking for their opinion is not weak; it is sensible, and it serves to empower that team member. The more facts you have the easier and more effective your decision-making will be. Getting the most out of your team is greatly aided by effective consultation and it demonstrates respect from you to them.

Training

Training is a boon if it is relevant to the team members receiving it. You are guaranteed to alienate staff by sending them on courses that bear no relevance to their role. Training for the sake of training is counter-productive. You need to ask: Will the training help the business? Is it geared to the priorities of the business? Are the right individuals and teams within your organization receiving the training? How can I quantify any improvement?

Training must be organized and delivered effectively or you should not commit to it in the first place. Ensure that the agreed priorities are met. Once this happens, think how you can help individual team members in their personal development. This can be a real aid towards improving performance and motivation.

When the training is over, try and evaluate its worth. Where do you expect to see improvements? If you evaluate effectively, you can judge where further investment in training will pay off.

Organizations of all sizes invest in their people through effective training. Your team is your most valuable asset and their performance has an impact on the company's bottom line.

All companies should review performance of their staff on a regular basis. When staff appraisals do not work, it is for the following reasons: There is no system in place for undertaking reviews on a regular basis; there is no paper trail to follow so people don't know where to start; they are used purely to air grievances so become a negative thing; the appraiser isn't trained to appraise so the results are unreliable; there is no follow-up so improvements are missed.

CHAPTER 4- LEADERS SHOULD LIVE BY EXAMPLE

Relationships can never improve unless problems are identified and confronted. Differences between people are inevitable, and hearing them aired can lead to some very useful resolutions that produce ideas beyond the expected. The alternative is highly detrimental: to let problems fester and build, and ruin the atmosphere in a workplace, if not productivity levels.

Keys for success in working relationships:

1. One party at least should value the relationship – This may start off as a one-way street, but this can lead to a meeting of minds later on.

2. Listen effectively, without judging – Listening in this way will promote mutual understanding and mutual respect.

3. Have informal chats – Chatting over a coffee can encourage a more frank exchange of views than meeting officially with a desk between you.

4. Create an open culture – Your team should know they can speak freely, no matter if that is to express happiness, joy, contentment, anger, irritation, sadness or fear. Negative feelings that are hoarded cause significant problems.

Change the Mindset

Leaders must take responsibility for their team's performance, which means leaders must be happy that the direction of their team is one which the leader thinks is best. Although it is useful to have creative sessions with team members to bat around a few ideas, the overarching goals that the team must fulfill are most often set by the leader, or some authority above the leader.

The challenge is therefore to get the team "onside" with the given aims, even when some team members may wholeheartedly disagree with them, or baulk at the idea that these have been imposed on them from above.

Despite the accepted hierarchy of any workplace, for a team to work most efficiently, its members – especially higher level ones – may want to feel they are contributing more than the spade work; they may like to feel that they have chosen where some of the plots should be dug.

This presents a challenge for the leader who cannot just let his or her subordinates have free play. The team must be made to feel involved and motivated. Or perhaps the situation is worse, and your team is beginning to show a little disobedience. How then to provoke a positive response in them?

The answer is by empowering your team, as far as possible. Short of handing over the reins and heading off home, the motivational leader must be able to create a sense that their team is actively involved in the process and contributing in a real sense to the overall outcome of the project.

This can involve learning how to make your suggestions appeal to them. This may mean you solicit their opinions and take the best ideas on board. Or you may have to convince them that your goals are shared and that their futures are tied to your overall success. It may be a simple matter of making an employee understand that their job will be safer if they perform well; reminding them that they are working for themselves and their family, and not just for a company.

However, empowering others does not just mean employing tactics that persuade other people to your own opinion or goals. It can also mean demonstrating leadership qualities that inspire others to act at their very best, no matter what is asked of them. Such leadership qualities would be most in evidence in the armed services, where the end result of potentially being killed is rarely going to elicit a whoop and a cheer. Soldiers are empowered to greatness by the examples set by their commanding officers.

Sometimes, it is just a matter of being an admirable and inspirational human being. Of course, some are born with more of these qualities than others, but we can all strive to lead by example, so that others will feel empowered to make great things happen.

CHAPTER 5- 10 EFFECTIVE LEADERSHIP TIPS

1. Ask to be judged

Finding out what others think of your leadership skills can really help you change for the better. Sometimes leaders can be so wrapped up in appraising others, that they do not seek appraisal from below, only from their own superiors. Your team is the best source of feedback, because they are on the receiving end of your "skills" every day.

Honesty should be encouraged, but bear in mind that it may only be anonymous feedback that holds the truth if your team believes you are going to use it against them, or become defensive about what they say. If you have created a trusting and open environment, this should not be a problem.

2. Don't abuse your power

If people are questioning why certain things are done, or the logic of decisions, never pull rank in response. Your team should feel empowered, if only by you taking the time to explain the rationale for any decisions that have been made. Your team must be on your side. This will not happen by you telling them that the decision is the right one because you are the boss. Your team may not agree, but they should know why a situation is how it is.

3. Your team is intelligent and can be trusted

Your team should be allowed to take actions and make decisions. Trust is a vital component of leadership skills. If you can't trust people to do their jobs, then you have the wrong people, or you're not managing them properly. Let them do what they are there to do without peering over their shoulders every fifteen minutes, asking what they are doing with their time.

4. Listen

Truly listening to your team is one of the greatest leadership skills. Good listeners come across as genuinely interested, empathetic, and concerned to find out what's going on. All great leaders have great communication skills.

Unhappy team members can only exist where their problems have not been aired. Create an environment where problems can be discussed so that solutions can be found.

5. Stop being an expert on everything

Leaders often achieve their positions by being proficient in a certain area, and thus will have an opinion on how to fix problems. They believe it's better to tell someone what to do, or even to do it themselves, than give their team the opportunity to develop their own solutions, and therefore exercise their creativity.

6. Be constructive

Negativity breeds negativity. How you communicate has a profound effect on your team, as a whole and individually. Criticisms will always need to be made by leaders, but try to make them constructive, and deliver them without emotional attachment.

7. Judge your success by your team's effort

The true success of a leader can be measured by the success of the people who work for them. You cannot be a successful leader of a failing team, just as you cannot be a successful general of a defeated army. Your focus should always be on building your team's skills and removing obstacles in their way.

8. Don't be a narcissist

Nothing is more annoying for team members than leaders who make their decisions based on how good it will make them appear to their superiors. A key leadership skill is integrity. Integrity is about doing the right thing, and allowing praise where praise is due, even if that is not at your door.

9. Have a sense of humor

People work better when they are enjoying themselves. The work itself may be dull, but the environment does not have to be. Stifling fun also means stifling creativity. Team members love it when the leader joins in and has fun. This does not have to create a flippant atmosphere; on the contrary, this is a tenet of team-building.

10. Don't be too distant

Without revealing you innermost secrets, it is possible for leaders to show a more human side. If mutual respect exists, this should not be seen as vulnerability, rather a sign that you are a sentient human being, just as your team members are. Only when your team gets to know the real you will the true foundations of good leadership be properly established – trust and respect.

Sun Tzu, writing in the 5th century BC in The Art of War said: "What enables the wise sovereign and the good general to strike and conquer and achieve things beyond the reach of ordinary men is foreknowledge."

This is an as-yet-unmentioned attribute of a great leader – the ability to predict. No matter how many managerial and people skills the business leader possesses, they will all be jeopardized if he or she cannot anticipate the effects of the plans they put in place, and the actions they take. In this respect, it may be that their age and experience must take precedence over consultation with the "troops", who may little understand the ramifications of what is about to take place.

This is where the genuine leader comes to the fore and truly claims their title. When all around are scratching their heads and reluctant to make a decision, old-style leadership must come into play. The modern leader may utterly fail in this scenario for lack of guts and an over-familiarity with their team.

As Sun Tzu says: "Some leaders are generous but cannot use their men. They love their men but cannot command them… These leaders create spoiled children. Their soldiers are useless."

Leadership may have become a different beast over the years, but it is still, at its heart, about leading.

With the help of this book you too can become a great leader. By following the leadership principles within you will be respected for your fairness, your skills and your ability to lead people in a humane but necessary way to achieve greatness with your team.

Leading people can be one of the most rewarding things you've ever done if you do it right. Do it wrong and leadership can quickly become a nightmare you hope to wake up from sooner than later.

Chapter 6- Leaders Motivate and Inspire People

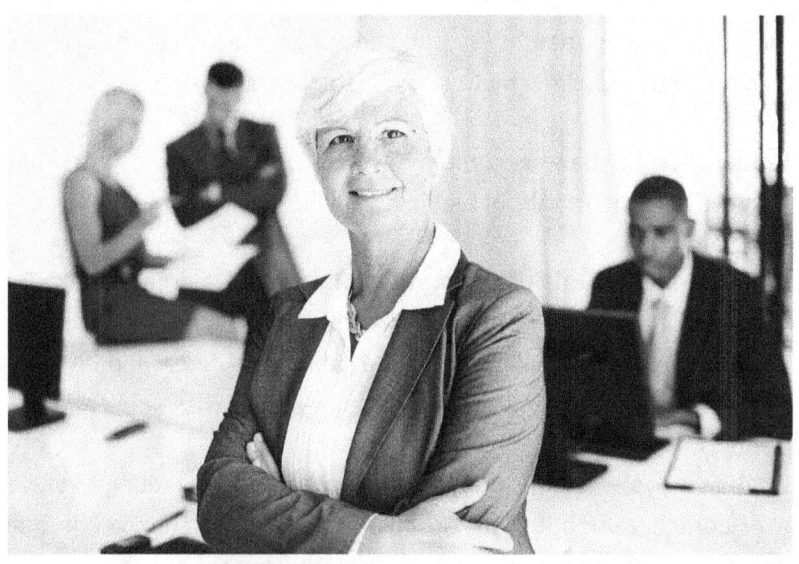

Successful leaders and managers today are willing to exercise their leadership in such a way that their people are empowered to make decisions, share information, and try new things. Most employees (future leaders) see the value in finding empowerment and are willing to take on the responsibilities that come with it. If future leaders have the wisdom to learn from the experience of present leaders, and if present leaders have the wisdom to build an environment that empowers people, both will share in the benefits.

Motivational problems can lead to performance issues that cost a business thousands of dollars in losses each year. A lack of motivation can lead to delays in the employee's completion of work and simple but expensive mistakes. By supporting and encouraging involvement, you are helping employees create a sense of connection that extends across departmental boundaries.

You can't lead without any people following you. You can't bring success to your business without motivated employees.

The vital key element of many successful companies, business, and organizations are their highly motivated employees. A company with motivated employees flourishes more. They get better leads and generate more sales.

Influential leaders and managers in today's world aim to exercise leadership where their people feel motivated and empowered to make right decisions, be assertive and cooperative as well as be engaging with trying out new things and sharing important information for the company.

Employees or the future leaders will see the value of motivations and find empowerment where they will find within themselves to responsible and creative with their tasks. If future leaders have the wisdom to learn from their present leaders and if present leaders have the wisdom to build an environment that empowers people, both will share in the benefits.

Motivation is the most powerful emotion and PUSH that employees bring to work. Every manager's commitment to motivating employees through shared vision and communication is the fundamental skill that great managers bring to the workplace. Employees with clear strategies and direction can work for you without much question ask.

Companies with motivational problems results in time to low performance issues that may affect the business to lose thousands of dollars of losses each year. A lack of motivation can lead to delays in the employee's completion of work and simple but expensive mistakes. By supporting and encouraging involvement, you are helping employees create a sense of connection that extends across departmental boundaries.

Goals and objectives of an organization whether a business or a team can only be fully achieved with the participation of active motivated efforts of the people. In order to do that, you're people should be fully motivated and excited to give their very best. However, as we all know, people are quite different from each other.

What motivates him might not motivate her at all, therefore, a manager or a leader should be open minded and understanding at all time as much as feasible as he can and be able to understand each and every member of his team or workplace.

Managers and leaders must strive to get the best of each person on their team or work group, which requires motivating different members in different methods while also motivating the whole team or group as a whole.

A motivated positive work environment factors on how you can motivate them. A trusting and cooperative working environment together with management and other personnel are required to create the environment for motivating people. The HR manager – along with other managers – has an important role to play in developing and maintaining a good work environment.

Motivated employees that are top grade professionals are quite hard to retain in companies because of today's cut-throat competition across industries and companies, and a broad of choices and offerings from companies and business, a high attrition rate is seen where employees will not hesitate to change jobs quick.

It's no wonder that a lot of companies are fighting hard to keep their employees stay within them while also pushing them to provide better performance.

Nowadays, even filling their pockets with healthy salary is not enough to retain them and keep them motivated and happy working at your company. Creating a positive environment is imperative for their well-being and also nurtures their talent.

Motivation may be essential to boost employees" performance better, but there is more. Having motivated employees can aid the growth and performance of an organization for the better.

Keeping employees motivated is vital for any business whether start-up, small or big successful businesses and franchises. Motivating your workforce means you can get highly productive and hardworking staff. This will help your business to achieve your goals and its target. This should be a main objective in your organizational and business plan.

Creating a motivational strategy will help you focus and strategically find effective ways to motivate your people, individually and as a whole but before you do this you have to understand or KNOW what drives your employees to perform well.

What motivate them to their peak performance will better help you develop programs that both motivate and retain the best employees for your business.

Remember as mentioned before, what motivates you might not motivate other people, but creating a list of effective of key motivating programs can help. Your plan can include everything from salary incentives, rewards and recognition, building programs that support work-life balance to simply creating a fun relaxed office environment. The opportunities are endless and the reward substantial.

One of the most popular methods is incentive programs. Any companies can easily use this to promote motivation on the workforce, but don't worry. Not all methods require overall monetary as solution. Small businesses usually suffer in this as having a tight budget, but the end results are the same; employees become more motivated when they are recognized and rewarded for good work.

Programs without high monetary incentives are quite common and they include not just bonus pools but also recognition like "Employee of the Month", to spotlighting employees on corporate websites or internal intranets. All will make employees feel connected, important and part of the success of the business.

You can also leave feedback for their annual reviews alone; it all depends on what motivational structure you'll use that will be effective. Just like any person, your employees would also feel the need to be recognized and appreciated, and even just passing by and taking time out to give a simple "thanks" or "great job" is another strong employee motivator. Frequently acknowledge good work.

They would want to feel appreciated of their good works and efforts. Your employees want and sometimes subconsciously seek face-to-face feedback from their managers. This should also include constructive criticism needed to address issues and help employees perform their jobs more effectively. While conducting formal reviews should be part of your ongoing strategy, periodic reviews and impromptu sessions will provide your employees with the feedback they need to succeed.

CHAPTER 7- GREAT LEADERS LISTEN TO THEIR PEOPLE

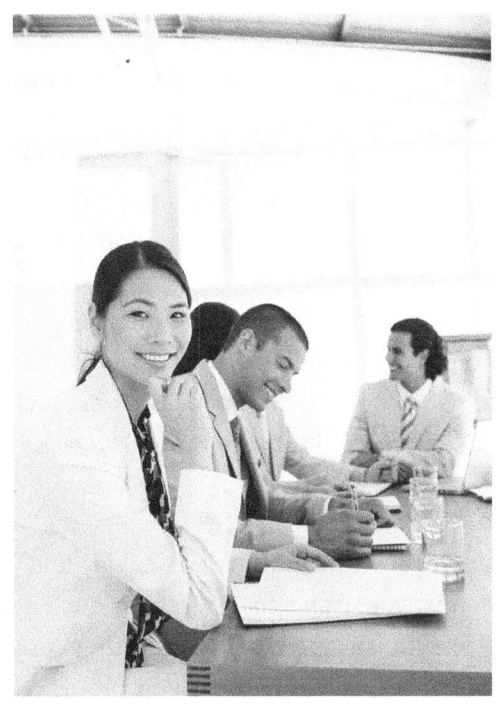

Encourage Feedback. Your employees need recognition. Giving them feedback time to time makes them feel and see that they are being heard within the team. This will help them feel that their opinions matter and they have a role in defining the success of your business.

Be POSITIVE. By the end of the day, what makes a company motivated and hardworking is the manager. It's your job and responsibility to create a positive environment for your employees. This can be accomplished by employing simple techniques from asking your receptionist to greet everyone with a smile, to encouraging employees to express their ideas openly.

The importance of employee motivation cannot be ignored or down-played. Ultimately when employees are motivated this increases productivity, lowers turnover and improves overall performance.

Why is employee motivation important?

The answer to "Why is employee motivation important?" is because in today's economy, it's more important than ever to have a motivated workforce rather than larger pool of employees.

The reason is quite simple: it's like having two new employees versus one professional employee. Though, with two heads, they might not be able to be as good and as productive as a professional. Likewise, a motivated employee is a productive employee.

Productive employees are more profitable and professional. Unmotivated employees tend to be less productive and creative making them less of an asset and losses their usefulness for a company. Now more than ever, we need motivated employees! Motivated employees are essential to all businesses.

What is Motivation?

Let's take motivation in a psychological perceptive and understand it. Motivation in all sense has different definitions and meaning in which most relates on how businesses or managers or leaders employ it.

Motivation is generally what energizes, maintains, and controls behavior; it acts as a stimulus for desirable actions. Motivation results in goal-directed behavior that results to a positive way of using energy and skills to toward a preferable outcome. The importance of this from a professional standpoint is enormous as much of what employees do is specifically delegated to capture present or future value for their company.

How important motivation is for a workplace is obvious and straightforward but can't be measured at all. Figuring out the level on how high motivation can result to higher productivity is difficult to pinpoint as what drives an individual is similarly difficult to measure. However, it is widely accepted and proven that motivated employees generate higher value and more substantial levels of achievement.

The management of motivation is, therefore, a critical element of success in any business, allowing the input of human resources to be maximized in regard to fulfilling the potential output expected.

Salary was once believed to keep an employee working for a company, but it does not mean that you are able to expand and use their abilities to its full potential. Herzberg's theory emphasizes that, while salary is enough to avoid dissatisfaction, it is not necessarily enough to propel employees to increase their levels of achievement.

Simply put it, understanding and knowing both internal and external motivations and also knowing the "needs" section is what can be valued. Furthermore, employees that are not motivated beyond the incentive of salary and benefits tend to decline in output over time. This fact lends strength to the argument that motivated employees are a critical aspect of a successful team or company.

"Actively disengaged employees erode an organization's bottom line while breaking the spirits of colleagues in the process. Within the

U.S. workforce, Gallup estimates this cost to be more than $300 billion in lost productivity alone. In stark contrast, world-class organizations with an engagement ratio near 8:1 have built a sustainable model using our approach. As organizations move toward this benchmark, they greatly reduce the negative impact of actively disengaged employees while unleashing the organization's potential for rapid growth."

– GALLUP

You can conclude that an "engaged" and "motivated" employee is a person who isn't just simply there to work but also a person who is fully involved in the company. They are excited about their work and will act and provide better performance for their organization's interests. According to Scarlett Surveys,

"Employee Engagement is a measureable degree of an employee's positive or negative emotional attachment to their job, colleagues and organizations that profoundly influences their willingness to learn and perform at work." (Scarlett, 2011)

Thus, engagement is a distinctive form employee satisfaction, motivation and organizational culture.

You might think that motivating people is easy as some may make it sound like, but in reality, it's quite hard and challenging. It needs clear thinking and hard work. Therefore, having the clarity of goals and expectations complemented by rewards, both tangible and intangible, motivates people to achieve organization goals.

1. Desire to be great

• People have a great desire to contribute to something lasting and get motivated naturally when they feel that they are working on something important, rare and marvelous.

2. Motivating by caring

• Showing genuine concern towards employees goes a long way in inspiring them. Whether it's spending on their ailing parent, sending a child to school or meeting their healthcare concern, it creates a sense of loyalty in the employees and thus helps in retaining them.

3. Motivating people at different levels

• Different people could be motivated at different motivation levels. This can also be based according to their skills. Some may want stock shares while others will only ask for bonuses depending on their contribution and position.

4. Motivating by setting difficult goals

• Difficult goals stimulate greater effort and greater performance. This linear relation could be explained by the following equation: Job performance = f (ability + knowledge) (Motivation). Abilities of a person could also be enhanced by the right motivation. This could be done by constantly exploiting the strengths of a person and ignoring his weaknesses.

5. Motivating problem people

• Understanding human nature becomes very critical in this regard. To motivate a problem employee, one should know what drives him. Then identify blocks to his drives and try removing those impediments.

More evidence supports that motivated employees provides:

- Finds better ways to do a job.

- They are quality oriented.

- Of course, they are more productive and efficient.

Overall, as stated many times, having motivated employees gives you high level innovation while they provide you with better higher quality of work at a high level of efficiency.

Though the benefits are quite broad, they are also quite vague that goes back whether the argument that motivated employees costs less and has no downsides. You can say that motivating employees cost NONE if the method you'll use requires no capital at all to coach managers to act as effective motivators.

Motivating people to take a risk can be truly challenging. This can be done by having a frank discussion on the chances of success, making roles & responsibilities clearer, spreading risk across the team and organization and by supporting the initiatives irrespective of the chances of success.

Effectiveness of people at the workplace depends on how their work will fit into the grand vision of organization and what the future holds for the organization and to them.

With the combination of recognition along with tangible rewards, the way motivation works is thus progressive and cumulative.

However, if this system is considered as a panacea, motivation may suffer badly. A suitable mix of rewards, incentives, and recognition augmented by a series of employee engagement activities must be integrated to retain people and encourage them to remain in the organization.

The most important factor in this mix should be "change". Therefore, excitement and fun and the thrill of new challenges keep the ball of motivation rolling. Even the best performance can be improved!

Chapter 8- Leaders: How to Be Firm with a Soft Heart

Many different things and factor can motivate a person in the workplace, but there are also different factors that can also motivate conflict and inflict stress in the workplace. One key factor is stress management, how the person handles stress is what will make or break a working relationship.

There are three main key theories that suggest how people reacts and pushes people to have the initiative or motivation or drive to do their job well and better while also relieving stress on the workplace.

Before we tackle the different theories of motivating employees in the workplace, let's find out why is it important to emphasize and create a process of motivation.

Any organizations flourish with employees. It's the most important part for any organizations. Without them, there's is no one to do the selling. Managers have been long known to think creative ways to keep employees motivated and hard working. Making sure they come to work regularly and energetic and continuously providing work that are positive contributions for the company.

When they are so, the business will be able to save up and cut costs while able to make more profit, which is the goal of any business or organizations built.

Unmotivated employees are what you can say a bit of a challenge to handle. Though they are qualified to their work, they are less likely to work on it. They are not willing to do well in their jobs or sometimes organizations will even require hiring other people to do different jobs that sadly results to high operating costs and reduction on profit which are not in favor for the company as well as the employees.

According to an article entitled „Need-based Perspectives on Motivation" by Moorhead and Griffin, job performance depends on three main factors: Motivation, Ability and Environment. In order for an employee to reach a higher level of performance, he/she must „want to do the job" (motivation), „be able to do the job" (ability), and „must have the materials, resources, and equipment to do the job" (environment).

"Performance = Motivation + Ability + Environment"

As stated above, within those three factors, motivation is simply the hardest and most difficult factor to manage and apply. This is basically due to the fact that a person's attitude and behavior are simply too complicated. It's filled with complexities and fallacies thus making it hard to categorize and to manage.

While the other two factors – Ability and Environment – are things that employee understands that he/she has been recruited for and has the awareness that he/she has the skills and capacity needed to perform the tasks as well as the fact that resources are readily available and if a manager sees that an employee lacks certain aspects of the job, he or she can provide training programs to learn that particular skill to be more efficient for the company.

If, however, an employee isn't suitable for the job or lacks hereof, the knowledge and ability for the job, there are other jobs that he/she can do, but if other resources are not available (the environment factor) the manager can take action to ensure that they become available.

For example, if an employee needs a photocopier, he/she can formulate request to the management team and ask for one. For this reason, it is quite clear that the most challenging job for every employer is how to motivate their employees to strive their best to work for the organization.

But if other resources are not available (the environment factor) the manager can take action to ensure that they become available. For example, if an employee needs a photocopier, he/she can formulate request to the management team and ask for one. For this reason, it is quite clear that the most challenging job for every employer is how to motivate their employees to strive their best to work for the organization.

Intrinsic Motivation Theory

Intrinsic Motivation Theory is used by "management teams" to motivate people with intrinsic rewards. Under this theory employees desire to do a good job because they are proud of what they are doing, and want to be a part of something good. For example, a Disney Imaginer feels satisfaction when he or she creates a new ride. The feeling of being a part of something so spectacular motivates him or her to do a great job.

Theory of Scientific Management

The Theory of Scientific Management has a unique view on how workers are motivated. It suggests that workers are motivated by what they produce, on their productivity while Intrinsic Theory suggests that they are motivated to do a great satisfying job. It states that workers aims to produce a lot of products in a specific period of time.

To put it simply, workers are paid more if they are more productive. This theory is often used for businesses since they require high productivity and mass production. However, overuse of this theory also conclude that employees will soon feel they are machines rather than co-workers which in turn result to dissatisfaction which is why the Intrinsic theory promotes a happier workplace than the Scientific Management Theory.

Motivation-Hygiene Theory

Similar to the Intrinsic Theory, the Motivation-Hygiene Theory suggests motivation through pride but rather than result-oriented, this theory states about employees pride through proper hygiene and appearance. Though this theory is still not completely proven to motivate employees, how they look and how they manage their

Leadership Made Easy

hygiene it is, in fact, helps increase self-esteem that does help for better performance. The best motivator though is the pride an employee takes in a job well done.

Employees that are too stressed out results to lower quality and productivity. Stress can also result to illness which can either be physical, like fatigue, or mental like anxiety and tension. However, a certain amount of stress is required to keep employees motivated. If things run too smoothly, employees can become inattentive and bored to do their work.

The Expectancy Theory

In this theory, both Maslow's and Herzberg's motivation theories presents that motivations is triggered by expectations. Though this is true in some points, by generalizing it both theories are criticized. It is obvious with many other recent researches that „the same people are motivated by different things at different times and that different people are motivated by different things at the same time. Therefore, there is no certain category of motivation. Expectancy" refers to the subjective probability" that one thing will result in another. Individual perception is, therefore, an essential part of Expectancy theory.

With this theory, an expectancy model was designed and here determined that one's motivation is strengthened as their perceived effort-performance and performance-reward probabilities increase. It may seem quite complicated, but we can discuss it through examples.

For instance, how strong can you be motivated to study if you expect to score poorly on your tests no matter how hard you study (low effort-performance probability) and when you know that the tests will not be graded (low performance-reward probability)? In contrast, your motivation to study will increase if you know that u can score well on the tests with just a little hard work (high effort-performance probability) and that your grades will be significantly improved (high performance-reward probability).

Employees and staffs are no different from students or any other people. They are simply motivated to do and work harder if it will give them better and more valuable rewards.

With this, an employee's contribution is determined on their rewards expectation. With this said, managers and leaders can create strategies to try to push them to work harder by making favorable expectations for their employees. When people can expect personally valued rewards, they will undoubtedly work harder to try to accomplish their tasks.

This is where one qualities of managers must have that will help; listening. One must listen to his/her employees, remember what they experienced as an employee and discover what rewards certain employees" value. So the manager can potentially enhance their employees" willingness to put more efforts into their work.

The Goal Setting Theory

Another theory is the Goal Setting Theory wherein as stated and developed both by Lotham and Locke in the year 1979 that a certain level of motivation and performance is higher when the individual has specific objectives established and when these objectives, even with a high level of difficulty, are accepted and are offered performance feedback.

The employees must participate in the process of goal setting in order to obtain their approval when setting higher and higher targets and the human resources people can help them to understand the consequences of these targets over their entire activity. Feedback is also vital to maintain the employee's motivation, especially when targeting even higher objectives.

Adam's Equity Theory

Categorized as one of the "justice" theories, The Equity Theory which was first developed and studied by John Stacey Adams claims and states that through satisfying the needs of fairness and equality brought upon by managers are a drive that brings out the best results from his/her employees. Equity theory places value on fair treatment.

An individual will consider that he is treated fairly when he feels that the he receives the amount similar to his output and it is the same to other people around him. In this case, it would be acceptable for an employee who has much more work experience and who is a more senior colleague to receive higher compensation/salary for his/her job.

However, if an employee feels that another individual who is as skillful as him and provides the same effort and output but earning more recognition or compensation, he will feel he's treated unfairly and thus perform at a lower level on his tasks.

An employee who feels he is over-compensated may increase his effort, but, he may also change the perceptions of his inputs and feel a sense of superiority, which may lead to him decreasing his efforts instead.

Theories of Motivation:

How to Use it on Practice

From theory to actual practice, motivation strategies are important. Though, applying which theory to use is quite tricky, however, practicing each varies depending on its application and to whom you are applying it with, in this case the employees.

Do they respond to praises and appreciations? Do they tend to respond on relaxed hours and a relaxed dress code? To structure and advertised perks related to performance?

Try understanding each theory by applying it to the workplace. You can try testing them all out and see which theory best works for the workplace and the employees within it.

Have an effective Reward System

Rewards are a great way to reinforce motivation in an employee's behavior and productivity. A reward is a work outcome of positive value to the individual. It's common for many organizations and companies to have a reward system given to those employees who exerts excellent performances, accomplishing great deals that are proving worth for the company's ideals. There are two types of reward system.

Extrinsic rewards are rewards and motivators that are received "externally". These are rewards given to employees when one's outcomes are perceived as great and best and usually given by managers or supervisors. Examples of extrinsic rewards are pay bonuses, promotions, time off, special assignments, office fixtures, awards, verbal praise, and so on. In all cases, the motivational stimulus of extrinsic rewards originates outside the individual.

Intrinsic rewards are something that comes from the "inside". These are rewards that make a person feel "special" or "high" after completing a job. That person feels good because she has a feeling of competency, personal development, and self-control over her work. In comparison with extrinsic rewards, intrinsic is compelled not by actions of other people.

Redesigning Jobs

Though jobs and employment are important, people who goes to their work every day doing the same thing makes the job seems mundane and boring. According to some individuals who experience this called it as "burnout". This is common to any company either small or large companies, but a smart manager can handle this situation if he knows what he's going to do.

The concept of job redesign, which requires understanding for the human qualities people bring with them to the organization, applies motivational theories to the structure of work for improving productivity and satisfaction.

When redesigning jobs, managers look at both job scope and job depth. Redesign attempts may include the following:

Job Enlargement

Job enlargement isn't adding more tasks but simply setting up lists of varieties of tasks that are included in their employment. It doesn't increase the job nor the quality and even the difficulty but instead decreases boredom and monotony of the tasks at hand. With this, it helps decrease inactivity and increase work quality of productivity.

Job rotation

This method allows people to experience different tasks in the company. This is, however, not permanent but rather allows employees to be exposed on the company's other jobs and also add variety and decrease boredom on employees. Job rotation can encourage higher levels of contributions and renew interest and enthusiasm. The organization benefits from a cross-trained workforce.

Job enrichment

This is also called vertical job loading but beside adding or giving a variety of tasks to an employee it also includes added responsibility and more authority. If the skills required to do the job are skills that match the jobholder's abilities, job enrichment may improve morale and performance.

Creating flexibility

Personal Time: Employees also requires this and fights for it. They need for many reasons such as family time and emergencies. The traditional nine-to-five workday may not work for many people anymore. That's why give "flextime". This gives employees the choice to set and control their own working hours. It's a sure method for any companies to be accommodating to his employees. Here are some other options organizations are trying as well:

A compressed workweek is a form of flextime that allows a fulltime job to be completed in less than the standard 40-hour, five-day workweek. Its most common form is the 4/40 schedule, which gives employees three days off each week. This schedule benefits the individual through more leisure time and lower commuting costs. The organization should benefit through lower absenteeism and improved performance. Of course, the danger in this type of scheduling is the possibility of increased fatigue.

Job sharing or twinning occurs when one fulltime job is split between two or more persons. This often happens when there are employees working for half day, but it can also be done on weekly or monthly depending on sharing arrangements decided.

When jobs can be split and shared, organizations can benefit by employing talented people who would otherwise be unable to work fulltime. For example, parents or mothers who need to take care of their children or their elders that are willing to work half-day. Although adjustment problems sometimes occur, the arrangement can be good for all concerned.

Telecommuting, sometimes called flexi place, is a work-arrangement that allows at least a portion of scheduled work hours to be completed outside of the office, with work-at-home as one of the options. Telecommuting frees the jobholder from needing to work fixed hours, wearing special work attire, enduring the normal constraints of commuting, and having direct contact with supervisors. Home workers often demonstrate increased productivity, report fewer distractions, enjoy the freedom to be their own boss, and appreciate the benefit of having more time for them.

Of course, when there are positives, there are also negatives. Many home workers feel that they work too much and are isolated from their family and friends. In addition to the feelings of isolation, many employees feel that the lack of visibility at the office may result in the loss of promotions.

There is no limit and different factors on how to motivate your employees on the workplace. A manager's responsibility is to understand his employees' needs and find effective ways to relieve their stress and make their daily working lives more relaxed and comfortable. All of these things will make for a pleasant and more productive workplace.

Chapter 9- Company's Interest is Leader's Goal

Put yourself on your employee's shoes, or just remember the time when you're not the manager. When your work isn't noticed or appreciated you feel that you're just a disposable employee of the company wherein they can replace you anytime.

If that's the case, then that's a workplace you'll definitely want to leave anytime.

This is not the type of working environment we or any managers want to implement and encourage on the workplace since the main goal is to motivate and retain professional employees and them providing excellent results.

So, as managers, one of your main responsibilities is creating a positive working environment wherein your employees will feel valued and appreciated. An environment wherein they can feel they are needed and contributing to the success of the company.

In today's modern employment system, you can easily find new employees either fresh graduates or professionals, however, getting them working while being involve for the benefit of both the company or organization and themselves can be quite a difficult task.

That said, when an employee feel that he/she is contributing to the welfare of the company or business, they are likely happier with their position and will stay loyal and to the company and producing more and higher quality of work.

Creating change to employee initiative and motivation can be quite hard especially when your employees have already settled down with the environment and the system the company uses. Shifts in marketing and sales strategy, management structure, workplace technologies or other areas can alter a business drastically.

Changes in the company whether small or fundamental may change how your employees will handle their responsibilities requiring them in some cases to learn new skills to remain productive. Change can also add stress. Psychological stress can build up as employees and staff must compromise and adjust to the changes and meet the needs of the company. For all these reasons, it's vital to inspire employees to work for change rather than against it.

Studies show that high-involvement work practices can develop the positive beliefs and attitudes associated with employee engagement. These practices also show that it also generates different kinds of discretionary behaviors that lead to enhanced performance. Simply put, employees who conceive the design and implement workplace and process changes are engaged employees.

Leadership Made Easy

Employee involvement is crucial in motivating them while creating an environment wherein people have an impact on decisions and actions that affect their jobs.

However, getting employee involvement isn't a goal or a tool for companies and organizations but rather a philosophy. It's leadership and management philosophy on how people responds and contributes to continuous improvement and the ongoing success of their work organization.

It can be critically important to competitiveness in the contemporary business environment. Employee engagement was positively associated with performance in a variety of areas, including increased customer satisfaction, profitability and productivity, and reduced employee turnover.

The breadth of employee involvement was substantial. About 2/3 of the business units scoring above the median on employee engagement also scored above the median on performance, while only about 1/3 of companies below the median on employee involvement scored above the median on performance (Harter, Schmidt & Hayes, 2002).

There are 3 main related components when it comes to employee involvement: a cognitive, an emotional, and a behavioral aspect.

Cognitive Aspect –concerns employees" beliefs about the organization, its leaders, and working conditions.

Emotional Aspect – concerns how employees feel about each of those three factors and whether they have positive or negative attitudes toward the organization and its leaders.

Behavioral Aspect – concerns about the value-added component for the organization and consists of the discretionary effort engaged employees bring to their work in the form of extra time, brainpower and energy devoted to the task and the firm.

Getting employees to be involved when it comes to the company's welfare such as decision making is important to continue the improvement and success of the business. Using strategic methods like employees suggestion systems, manufacturing cells, work teams and events you can employ involvement into employees. Other methods can include Kaizen (continuous improvement) events, corrective action processes, and periodic discussions with the supervisor.

Being good in business calls on being good at being human," Petzinger concludes after studying the turnaround of Rowe Furniture Company. Rowe, which had been a very traditional manufacturing company, identified the need to utilize the brains and talent of its employees. Charlene Pedrolie, its manufacturing chief, truly believed that the people doing the work should design how the work is done.

With the assistance and consultation from a much reduced management team and engineers, workers redesigned their work. They moved from an environment in which each person handled part of a work process to fully cross-trained manufacturing cells producing a whole product.

From standing at an assembly position all day long, they created work which allowed some freedom and movement. They eliminated the formerly "deadly dull" jobs. At the same time, the flow of information they received, which allowed them to know exactly how they were performing, increased dramatically.

Leadership Made Easy

The new sense of personal control, according to Petzinger, "bred a culture of innovation in every corner of the planet..." It reveals the creative power of human interaction.

It suggests that efficiency is intrinsic; that people are naturally productive; that when inspired with vision, equipped with the right tools, and guided by information about their performance, people will build on each other's action to a more efficient result than any single brain could design.

Employee Involvement Model

As mentioned, there are different methods to apply to instill employee involvement. Different models can be used. One of the best tried, and tested model was developed from research theories from Tannenbaum and Schmidt (1958) and Sadler (1970). They suggest that through continuous proper leadership plus involvement increases the chance of employees motivations making them take more roles willingly and decrease role of supervisors with the decision process.

Tell: the supervisor makes the decision and announces it to staff. The supervisor provides complete direction.

Example: Useful when communicating about safety issues, government regulations, decisions that neither require nor ask for employee input.

Sell: the supervisor makes the decision and then attempts to gain commitment from staff by "selling" the positive aspects of the decision.

Example: Useful when employee commitment is needed, but the decision is not open to employee influence.

Consult: the supervisor invites input into a decision while retaining authority to make the final decision herself.

The key to a successful consultation is to inform employees, on the front end of the discussion, that their input is needed but that the supervisor is retaining the authority to make the final decision. This is the level of involvement that can create employee dissatisfaction most readily when this is not clear to the people providing input.

Join: the supervisor invites employees to make the decision with the supervisor. The supervisor considers her voice equal in the decision process.

The key to a successful join is when the supervisor truly builds consensus around a decision and is willing to keep her influence equal to that of the others providing input.

Delegate: the supervisor turns the decision over to another party.

Employee Satisfaction Research

In a study, The Impact of Perceptions of Leadership Style, Use of Power, and Conflict Management Style on Organizational Outcomes by Virginia P. Richmond, John P. Wagner, and James McCroskey, the researchers developed an instrument to measure employee satisfaction using this continuum (tell, sell, consult, join).

Their research discovered, "the supervisor who wishes to generate a positive impact on satisfaction with supervision, satisfaction with work, and solidarity and to reduce communication anxiety should strive to get her/his subordinates to perceive her/him as using a more employee-centered (consult-join) leadership style." At the same time, however, the supervisor cannot be seen by employees as abdicating responsibility for decision-making.

The authors further concluded, "We believe there is a relatively straightforward explanation of this finding. Leadership styles, which approach the employee-centered (join) end of the continuum, increases the degree to which subordinates are asked to participate in making decisions and/or make the decision themselves.

When this approach becomes excessive, the supervisor may be seen as abdicating her/his responsibilities-the laissez faire leader-or even deserting the subordinate. The subordinate may feel that they are given more responsibility than their positions should require and, thus, are overworked or underpaid for the work expected.

Such reactions could be expected to be reflected in negative outcomes of the type observed in this study. We conclude that while the supervisor should attempt to be perceived as employing an employee-centered leadership style (consult-join), he/she must maintain a supervisory role and avoid being perceived as abdicating responsibility."

Employee Involvement for Effective Change Management

Create a plan for involving as many people as possible, as early as possible, in the change process.

Involve all stakeholders, process owners, and employees who will feel the impact of the changes, as much as possible, in the learning, planning, decisions, and implementation of the change. Often, in change management, a small group of employees learns important information about change and change management. If they fail to share the information with the rest of the employees, the remaining employees will have trouble catching up with the learning curve.

If a small group makes the change management plans, employees affected by the decisions will not have had needed time to analyze, think about, and adjust to the new ideas. If you leave employees behind, at any stage of the process, you open the door in your change management process, for misunderstanding, resistance, and hurt.

Even if employees cannot affect the overall decision about change, involve each employee in meaningful decisions about their work unit and their work.

Build measurement systems into the change process that tell people when they are succeeding or failing. Provide consequences in either case. Employees who are positively working with the change need rewards and recognition. After allowing some time for employees to pass through the predictable stages of change, negative consequences for failure to adopt the changes, are needed.

You cannot allow negative-minded people to continue on their path forever; they sap your organization of time, energy, and focus, and eventually, affect the morale of the positive many. The key is to know, during your change management process, when to say enough is enough.

Help employees feel as if they are involved in a change management process that is larger than themselves by taking these actions to involve employees effectively in change management.

So just how do you get employees more involved in company decisions?

Increasing COMMUNICATION is one of the best ways to do so. Suggestion boxes are a popular method. It works best since they are named anonymous, and whether it's a simple suggestion or not feasible, it is recognized. If an employer does not address every suggestion then participation will taper, and efforts will be futile. Employee surveys help gain feedback and involvement.

These surveys should ask probing questions that invite employees to give feedback rather than just bubble in a meaningless "strongly agree." A final way to open communication is to talk to employees.

You can implement annual reviews as a formal evaluation of the employee's work. This includes everyone. Just as employees are told what they can do better, employees should be invited to tell managers what improvements they would like to see. Nevertheless, as managers continue to open up communication to one another, a great shift of improvement that values feedback will in turn make employees naturally motivated to be involved and work harder.

Self-management is another method to make employees involved. Nobody likes being micro-managed, or even hearing suggestions as to where their priorities should be.

Some companies do this by allowing employees to manage their own time (depending on the nature of the job). They don't need to work at strict 8 hours of continuous job but instead get breaks or early day offs without informing managers.

Not only it decreases stress it also allows work-life balance. It is important with the self-management system that employees are well aware that they are not an island. Allowing employees to work in this way automatically encourages them to be more involved in day-to-day operations.

Other methods for employee involvement are emphasizing COMMUNICATION and TRUST. Managers are required to listen and trust his employees on how they handle their works, of course, with guidance.

The next time they are asked for feedback they will be willing give it because managers will have proven that they value it. So have a little faith, try a little more hands-off guidance, and you may be surprised at how willing people are to step up and be involved.

Chapter 10- The Power of Reward System

Theories and research suggest and been proven that without giving out praise and recognition to employees are one of the main reasons they leave certain companies and organizations.

Though increasing salary and adding bonuses are already important motivators, companies must also recognize employees" achievement for the company at least once or twice a year. You can do this in different ways. Events and celebrations showcasing and awarding achievement of employees or teams are one way to do it or give added rewards for their achievement.

Peter Drucker said that leadership is that quality of examining work to ensure that effort is not placed where there are no results.

According to this definition, leadership is the skill of establishing priorities and marshaling resources to achieve worthwhile goals. While some may disagree with this definition, few will argue that Drucker's view is unreasonable.

Supervisors have the difficult and primary task of determining what is important in their organization. Drucker advises them to forget about yesterday's services, to maintain today's breadwinners and, as managers, to emphasize and nurture tomorrow's objectives. Indeed, a fundamental rule of leadership is to delegate yesterday and undertake tomorrow.

Those expensive experiences in management ego, in developing and maintaining services and collections long after analysts have revealed their failure, must be avoided. Leadership is the art of recognizing the mistake, even one's own, and correcting it before it bleeds the institution.

The leader is also the person who must ask himself and the members of his administrative team to redefine the purpose and role of their institution regularly. The leader must clarify the institution's goals and objectives and remind his team of those ends. To be successful, the leader must ensure that the team knows both the goals and strategy. (Excerpt from SUPERVISION OF EMPLOYEES IN LIBRARIES: Leadership and Employee Motivation by Donald J. Sager; page 45- 46)

Leaders today must learn and master new skills adding up to the traditional leadership methods to lead their teams and employees into the success of the company. Continuously mentioned in this book is that motivating employees is imperative and thus a skill any leaders must acquire. It can be quite costly but with the right usage of tools can be advantageous for all and most organizations.

Leadership Made Easy

Leaders must employ these tools and resources properly to achieve their goals.

When it comes to motivating employees, one leadership trait to have is the ability to infuse inspiration to each member/staff or employees. Besides sharing ones' vision and directions, asking for opinions and ideas is a great way to build trust and relationship as well as inspire each other. It can be called as "successful leadership relationship" and must be effortless when it comes to inspiring employees. Following an effective leader, people accomplish and achieve more than they may ever have possibly dreamed.

The foundation of this successful relationship is the leader's ability to make people feel important. So, effective leaders need to demonstrate these practices.

Pay attention to people using common courtesy. Simply saying "Good Morning" or replying to each courtesy will inflict positive feedback. Asking how their weekend was or their family is a powerful simple tool to practice to in order to build relationships toward your people.

Listen to your people. Rather than leading and them listening only to you, the leader, start listening to your employees/staff or members and give full attention when needed. Set meetings to listen to their needs better.

Moreover, you can hear more of their ideas and opinions regarding the organization and oversee which and what is working for their comfort. You make people feel special when you listen to them without distraction Positive, powerful languages. A simple "Thank you" or "Great Job" is a positive and powerful phrase to say to your employees that can impact their daily lives into positive ways. It encourages them to work harder and better for the company's and their welfare. Other phrases can include but not limited to, "Your contribution saved the customer for the company." "We couldn't have accomplished the goal without you."

Put praise in writing. A "thank you" note to the employee, with a copy to her file, magnifies the impact of the recognition.

Keep true to commitments. Make sure never to cancel except in a true emergency. Promising raise or bonus? Never fail it. Do not keep promises or commitments you can't meet.

Give credit to employee contribution. Remember suggestion boxes and meetings? When a great idea is presented, make or suggested it.

When fulfilling responsibilities as a leader, it is quite obvious that most are no longer willing or motivated to work. This is not necessarily either good or bad. Employing cheap and willing labor is no longer easy like what most companies are used to. Even employing student labor isn't as many as before and commonly most students are no longer willing to work extra and do mundane work such as categorizing and shelving files and books. They will work, but prefer to do so in areas where they can gain useful experience for their own careers.

"Too often the solution seems to be a higher salary, but this is not necessarily so."

Most people and even companies" think that money is already a good motivator for employees to stay in their companies most simply pretends but if you change the reward, you can change people's behavior.

Some researchers argue that to motivate employees you should be able to give them happiness. However, Duke Psychology Professor Dan Ariely argues that both happiness and money are both motivators and simply categorizing them based on money and happiness will oversimplify things and miss out the important factors on what motivates people.

Many people think that, in the end, motivation is all about money, for all that people pretend otherwise. If you change the reward, you can change people's behavior.

Others argue that it's all about finding happiness. Duke psychology professor Dan Ariely argues that both play a part but that those explanations wildly oversimplify things, and miss out on what truly motivates people.

In a recently posted TED talk, he points to finding meaning in work, and being able to see progress as extremely important motivators.

This means managers play a huge role in the quality and quantity of someone's everyday work, and that they have to be very conscious of their behavior. "Ignoring the performance of people is almost as bad as shredding their effort in front of their eyes,"Ariely says.

Nothing destroys people's confidence and motivation more than busy work, and nothing gets them going more than constantly seeing their progress and caring about it.

In an experiment, Ariely had participants build a series of Lego figures, paying them successively less for each one. Group A had their finished figures put under the table and were told they would be broken down later. Group B had their work broken down right in front of them, and had the disassembled pieces given back to them if they chose to build another one.

The difference in meaning was small. Both figures would end up being broken down. It made a big difference in people's motivation and willingness to work. The Group A built 11 figures on average, and Group B, 7.

Not only that, the latter condition made even people who loved building Lego dramatically less productive.

This translates directly to the workplace. Ariely once spoke at a Seattle-based software company, to a team that had been given the task of innovating the next big product for a company. A week prior to Ariely's visit, the CEO canceled the project.

An acknowledgment is essential and even the briefest notice and attention makes a huge difference. It's about remembering workers are humans, not machines.

Money is a powerful lever, but it's not the only one. The best managers and companies figure out how to use everything.

Recognize Employees

One method that most leaders and managers often forget is to recognize the efforts and achievement done by employees. Employee recognition goes a long way toward increasing and maintaining achievement.

Studies show that when employees feel valued or recognized with their achievement and the contribution, they are more likely to strive more and desire to contribute more for the success of the company. Managers who never thank their employees can cause a decline in motivation.

It's not important to give extravagant gifts, but rather just the thought of being recognized is motivation enough. Other ways to recognize employees include a paid day off, a card expressing gratitude and flexibility in work schedules.

Rather, employee recognition is better and more effective when it is done with sincerity, and if you are giving them fair wages rather than just increasing their salaries.

Quality of Life

Having a comfortable working environment and understanding employee needs has shown increase productivity with higher results. It's a common issue and problems for employees to manage and balance both work and personal lives that may affect negatively to their morale and work performance.

Managers and leaders can give comfortable working place by implementing flexible working schedules/hours or the schedule to be able to work home. Incorporating quality- of-life strategies in the workplace allows employees to remain focused on completing their duties.

Provide Personalized Coaching

It's normal that not all employees already knows and understands how the company system works and this may demotivate them. Implementing coaching and seminars can improve their skills and increase their performance that will give higher results.

A primary way to help employees improve their performance is to offer feedback. Rather than after they complete a task, provide feedback before the completion of theirs task. Managers should provide feedback based on actual performance and not biased opinions. When employees can sense biased opinions, they begin to lack motivation and work less. When providing feedback, an employer should listen and address the employee's concerns.

Monetary Incentives

Though non-monetary methods are good and effective methods to motivate employees, monetary incentives have been long known to play a huge part on one's motivation. Monetary incentives, such as profit sharing and performance bonuses, motivate employees to render quality products, high levels of productivity and innovative and creative processes.

With monetary incentives, it's proven that any companies and businesses benefit highly since it motivates employees to be more productive and efficient impacting the whole company's profit. However, relying solely on money incentives isn't enough to motivate employees. Using other methods will in a short time inspire motivation and employees will work harder and better.

Here are some tips to remember when it comes to employee recognition. Make sure to establish certain criteria for what you believe in as high performance and contribution wherein it is deemed reward-able whether behavior or tasks or the company.

All employees must be eligible for the recognition.

The recognition must supply the employer and employee with specific information about what behaviors or actions are being rewarded and recognized.

Anyone who can perform at the level or standard stated in the criteria receives the reward.

The recognition should occur as close to the performance of the actions as possible, so the recognition reinforces behavior the employer wants to encourage.

Reduce using selective employee recognition methods. It is viewed as a form of "favoritism" which can decline employee involvement and trust. This is why processes that single out an individual, such as "Employee of the Month" are rarely effective.

Attaching "true" accomplishments and goals to recognition and rewards in accordance to your set criteria decided through meetings, and performance development is something that organizations, whether small or large-scale should not overlook and simply choose.

Creating criteria and goals for either teams or individual employees and member accomplishments should be viewed through a series of processes for it to be a success.

Sometimes you can make quick simple recognition that can either be unique and random at some times. What matters is the element of surprise employees will receive.

Simple things like giving free meals sometimes a week is great but be careful as some might take advantage of it or rewarding beset decorations for the holidays.

Recognition and reward system are both beneficial for managers and employees. Plan out what you'll give as rewards and what to recognize.

Avoid the employee recognition traps that:

Single out a few employees who are mysteriously selected for the recognition,

Strengthen the morale of the many who failed to understand the criteria enough to compete and win, and

Sought votes or other personalized, subjective criteria to determine winners.

Here are some 9 methods to reward employees that as well show that you are seeing and recognizing their hard work and achievements.

Reward #1 Money

Give raises (equity, retention & reflection of work performed)

Re-class or Promote (equity, retention & reflection of work performed)

Give bonuses (Up to $200 in state funds per employee per year can be awarded for recognition purposes)

Pay the same salary but decrease FTE

Reward #2 Recognition

Nominate for awards

Give Awards

Extend personal congratulations for a job well done

Write personal note or letter of thanks (particularly from Deans & Chairs) and place in personnel file

Recognize individuals/teams at staff meetings or publicly in other ways

Hold meetings to celebrate successes

Throw parties for special events (i.e., Service Awards, Goodbyes, Accomplishments, and Awards)

Reward #3 Time Off

Professional Staff can be given up to 6 days discretionary leave off on an annual basis

Flex time (working core hours and work 8 hours/day but come in from 8 – 8:30 and leave from 4 – 4:30; not appropriate for all jobs)

Telecommute Days (not appropriate for all jobs)

Alternative Work Schedules (9/80s and 4/10s)

Release time for classes (as viable)

Reward #4 A piece of the action

Ask staff their opinions and ideas – individually and in meetings

Encourage their feedback

Have staff participate on committees and in meetings

Recommend individuals to others as a resource or

Subject matter expert (sme)

Assign staff projects which draw on their ideas & creativity

Have staff committees plan celebrations & holiday events

Listen (be available & accessible to staff)

Reward #5 Favorite work

Recognize staff's talents when assigning work projects

Let staff cross train on other functions

Assign staff to do some committee work

Rotate interesting projects among staff

Allow for some expansion of job duties (not necessarily an increase in complexity – which could lead to a re-class) which may break the monotony of a position and lead to greater job satisfaction

Reward #6 Advancement

Reclassify positions as appropriate

Provide tools and growth so that staff can advance

Talk to staff about their career goals and try to incorporate some into the job as appropriate and relevant

Empower staff to make decisions about their jobs and allow them to grow

Reward #7 Freedom

Allow for flexibility in work hours (staff should work core hours and 8 hours/day but come in from 8 – 8:30 and leave from 4 – 4:30). This may not be appropriate for all jobs

Allow for freedom to work independently (not micromanaged)

Understand that there are many different ways to accomplish tasks and allow for individual

Encourage their feedback

Have staff participate on committees and in meetings

Recommend individuals to others as a resource or subject matter expert (sme)

Assign staff projects which draw on their ideas & creativity

Have staff committees plan celebrations & holiday events

Listen (be available & accessible to staff) differences/creativity (focus on your expectations for the final outcome and timelines)

Reward #8 Fun

Provide lunches (pizza)

Have other food items at meetings, or for little gatherings (10 minutes):

Ice Cream Socials

Doughnuts

Bagels

Cake

Throw parties (for goodbyes, to celebrate service awards, for Staff Appreciation Day, etc.)

Provide opportunities to laugh and socialize

Reward #9 Prizes

Fun inexpensive prizes related to holidays are fun

Contests for teams or individuals who are working on finishing major projects, or eliminating backlogs

Lunch with someone in leadership position.

CHAPTER 11- HOW TO CREATE A POSITIVE WORKING ENVIRONMENT

Try making a simple survey by asking random people, let's say around 50 people, and ask them if they are fully engaged and motivated when working. Sadly, research shows that only less than 50% of them are not fully engaged. This obviously shows how employee talent and potential are gone to waste.

When employees are not fully engaged with their work, means they are not enjoying the working environment and simply can't give their 100% for every task whether given to them. The organization's performance remains a meager fraction of what it could be. This impact of disengaged employees on organizational performance will only increase as we move further towards a knowledge economy driven by human capital.

If spreading positive attitude in the workplace is successful then it decreases turnover, minimizes employee complaints and creates a positive working team that every member is excited to contribute.

Energy is everywhere around you. It can either be positive or energy, but it sure does define whether it will be to your success or promote your demise.

Everything you involve yourself in is a result of the energy you contribute. How well you act and contribute as a professional is also as important on what you contribute. You may be a professional, with higher knowledge and sets of skills and history of success, but if you approach a new job or a team or your boss or even your customer with negative energy then you should take full responsibility to the worse consequences of this action.

Experts claim that energy is neither or positive, and this is always neutral and will only be either positive or negative depending on which form we want it to be in which, in fact, true when it comes to the working environment and/or other places or organizations.

Negativity comes in many forms especially in the workplace (or anywhere for that matter). Spot negativity in many forms:

Complaining (this is huge)

Putting others down

Talking about people behind their back

Highlighting other people's mistakes (pointing the fingers of blame)

Focusing on / expecting the worst

The truth is as leaders and managers you have the power to exert and control your energy on how you let other perceives it but as well as receive and understand other's energy whether positive or negative.

Sometimes it is easy to see how others affect you, but many times you may not even realize the effect others had on you. Being aware on how people react to a certain situation and how they feel will decrease negative energy and promote positive energy.

As a manager, your energy is what determines the success of your team whether on meetings or on actual working hours. If you have an employee or co-worker who is struggling, have you considered how much responsibility you have in their performance?

If you were chosen to become the leader or manager or supervisor for other employees and members, your responsibility is to how you'll manage your own energy, as well as the negative energy from the employees.

Negative energy is contagious. It may seem as if dealing with negative people is easier to ignore them but their energy affects other people without them knowing it. Therefore, your negative employees may be consciously or sub-consciously expanding their negativity and influencing the behavior of others.

Managers and leaders look on what is happening. Are you contributing positively to the welfare of your company? Is your energy affecting both your personal and professional life? How do you handle your employees? Do you do so professional while being responsible? Are you POSITIVE when it comes to your work? Does your workplace have a POSITIVE environment, comfortable for working?

Start with Yourself!

Inspiring positive energy in the workplace starts with one's self. When questioning whether you are positively on the right direction in the workplace try asking yourself these following questions:

Are you generally a positive or negative person?

Do you have a high or low energy level?

How do others respond to you; relaxed or tense?

Do you find yourself being judgmental of others or open and accepting of diversity and new ideas?

Do you harbor anger rather than letting these feeling go?

Do you feel mostly happy or sad and frustrated?

Are you a nice person?

Be Aware of your ENERGY

Being aware of how you emit your energy to the workplace is the key to improve the workplace energy. Managers and leaders should aim to create a positive working environment to keep employees motivated and engaged at their works. That's why by simply taking the time to observe others both your employees and staff, you may create a new awareness of the type of energy that is most common in your department or company.

Negative Energy, Stay Away!

How you handle your energy and how well you observe your employees energy can be determined on how well your employees perform.

Since employees work their whole day almost in the workplace, they will want to feel comfortable and relaxed even with the workload. Figuring out who has negative energy in the workplace won't be easily determined by their turnout but with how they socialize while working. In order to start creating a positive working environment, begin with one's self, affecting others for better.

However, if you identify a negative employee who is not supporting the environment you are expecting to create, it is critical to deal with this behavior.

Take necessary steps to help the employee feel comfortable in order to improve but if this employee refuse to be more positive and effective, then you can't simply ignore it. Allowing this employee to continue contributing negative energy will quickly infect the energy of other employees and you.

Set Expectations

Have your own management style and see if it works well with your employees. It should be able to create positive-minded employees with supportive and rewarding process. Reward the positive improvements and mentor the employees who are not exceeding expectations. It's great to reinforce positive energy continuously to build and maintain productivity momentum to reach your goal quicker with better results.

Energize you TEAM!

Working every day and doing almost the same things bore your employees and sap out their positive energy. Find fun great ways to boost them up even while doing meetings, meeting deadline and finishing projects. This can be as simple as frequent short breaks, laughter, creating a very open environment where fresh ideas and creativity is rewarded.

The relationships you align in life reflect who you are. You are defined by your relationships in your personal life and most certainly within your professional career. If you find the majority of your employees are tired, or your team is experiencing difficulty with exceeding expectations and creating momentum, seriously consider evaluating the energy flowing within your company. Do not wait for others to create the positive, rewarding, motivating environment since you already have that power to do so. A positive environment is a healthy environment.

As a manager or a leader as a team, it is your responsibility to take the initiative role to encourage positive energy in the workplace. It is a worthy investment of time and energy as it gives better results and productivity. Remember, that to spark initiative and positive energy takes one or two persons to start it. You, managers and leaders, should be the first persons to take the initiative.

Here are some ideas to spark positive energy and encouragement:

Showing Gratitude

Inspiring positive energy and encouragement can start by recognizing their contribution to the company. Simply saying "thank you" to each person can set a powerful builder motivating them to work harder and improve their work-life.

Focus on their skills

Improve yourself and others by focusing on one's skills and also incorporate them to each daily lives. You can also help them learn new skills needed for their task.

Balance negative energies

We are all people. We will and often times dwell to our negative energies. Most of the time, we tend to focus on goals and projects we haven't fulfilled or fear of the unknown future of the projects. Build your inner resilience by refocusing your energy on successes when you are faced with disappointment or stress.

Practice "flexible" thinking

When receiving new projects and challenges, instead of thinking of what might go wrong, embrace the new possibilities and potential obstacles with positive thinking. Manage them effectively and face the unexpected events without any problems.

Acknowledge steps to success

Large projects and tasks are often intimidating. Make it easier and fun by planning steps and dividing it too easy-to-handle tasks for employees and make goals achievable to maintain focus and balance energy.

TEAM Support

Leading and managing your employees requires supporting and trusting them with their skills while leading them to ensure productivity and quality.

Communication is important! If you feel less confident about them, they can sense it with your energy and often times will lead to negative energy and discouraged employees. Help them develop.

Now, here are some quick tips that you can DO NOW to promote positive energy to others. (Excerpt from 5 Ways to Create a Positive Workplace Atmosphere - Harriet Meyerson)

• Greet everyone today with an enthusiastic "Hello" and a smile and good eye contact. You will get some smiles back creating a positive connection, and positive energy.

• End every phone call and email with, "Have a great day." Your positive energy will come across, and both of you will feel energized.

• Give everyone a compliment. It's easiest to say something nice about what they are wearing. Even better, compliment, such as "You are so..."creative and detail oriented, dependable, etc"... that it makes my day so much more ..."pleasant, exciting, enjoyable," etc."

• Try baking some chocolate chip cookies and pass them out. Homemade cookies say, "I cared enough to take the time to make them." However, they are easy to bake because you can get the pre-mixed ones in squares at the grocery store, pop them in the oven, and in a few minutes you have a delicious cookie.

ABOUT THE AUTHOR

William "Billl" Groves has already proved himself as a successful entrepreneur and inter marketer. He knows that success can be achieved by all with the right mindset, attitude and determination. Bill has honed and developed his prolific leadership skills through his long years in managing teams.

Bill wants everyone to achieve a level of satisfaction in their own lives and does his best to help by equipping others with the right knowledge that they need to do so. Aside from a successful businessman and leader, Bill is also successful and happy as a father.

www.ingramcontent.com/pod-product-compliance
Lightning Source LLC
Chambersburg PA
CBHW071252170526
45165CB00003B/1309